Muscle Boats

The classic and the new wave: deep-vee hulls and catamarans

Henry Rasmussen

Motorbooks International
Publishers & Wholesalers Inc
Osceola, Wisconsin 54020, USA   ®

PRINTED IN HONG KONG

First published in 1988 by Motorbooks International Publishers
& Wholesalers Inc, P O Box 2, 729 Prospect Avenue, Osceola,
WI 54020 USA

Printed and bound in Hong Kong

The information in this book is true and complete to the best of
our knowledge. All recommendations are made without any
guarantee on the part of the author or publisher, who also
disclaim any liability incurred in connection with the use of this
data or specific details

We recognize that some words, model names and designations,
for example, mentioned herein are the property of the
manufacturers. We use them for identification purposes only.
This is not an official publication

Library of Congress Cataloging-in-Publication Data
Rasmussen, Henry.
  Muscle boats.

  1. Cigarette boats--Pictorial works.   I. Title.
VM341.R37 1988   387.2'31'0222   88-12860
ISBN 0-87938-312-7

Motorbooks International books are also available at discounts
in bulk quantity for industrial or sales-promotional use. For
details write to Special Sales Manager at Publisher's address

On the cover: Donzi's Z-33 Crossbow zooms through the
turquoise waters of Tampa Bay. **On the back cover:** two of
the premier muscle boats, the red Tempest Sport and the
white Cigarette Cafe Racer. **On the frontispiece:** the
Crossbow—Donzi's top-of-the-line thirty-three-footer—
looks like an all-devouring sea monster as it chases across
smooth Tampa Bay. **On the title page:** the wake of a
Cigarette at top speed—caught by the radar gun at 81
mph—cuts a clean furrow through the Intracoastal
Waterway. **On this page:** a collection of spare propellers
found at North Miami Beach's Fort Apache Marina. **On
the last page:** a Fountain clears its four wide throats,
producing jets of hot exhaust and cooling water.

Contents

Epic tale of deep-vee hulls and quadruple-digit horsepower

Today's muscle boat represents a relatively recent development. As such it is a product still in search of its ultimate form and potential, and in fact, it even lacks a universally accepted name. Runabout, the term used to describe the fast boats of the classic era, has a decidedly antiquated ring to it. Speedboat? Powerboat? Sportboat? All are too general. Cigarette? The appellation appeals to our vocabulary and has taken on something of a generic quality. Being an active trademark, however, it is never heard among people in the know.

Tracing its lineage to offshore racing, the modern muscle boat has become a symbol of the relentless quest for performance. These boats characterize the most voracious pursuers of life in the fast lane—perhaps even more so than the exotic automobile, whose territory has constantly been shrinking as a result of the ever-growing roadblocks of legislation.

There was a time when powerful automobiles ruled the roads. The zenith came during the sixties, with the rise and fall of the muscle car. Fortunately, the limitless freedom of that era can still be found on the high seas—there to be conquered by the fastest and the strongest. In this sense, the muscle boat is the inheritor of the muscle car legacy. Yet while the muscle car—with its affordability—was a machine for the masses, today's muscle boat—with its astronomical price tag—is just a toy for the privileged few.

The early period of motorized boating corresponds roughly to the pioneer days of the horseless carriage. And just as the automotive field

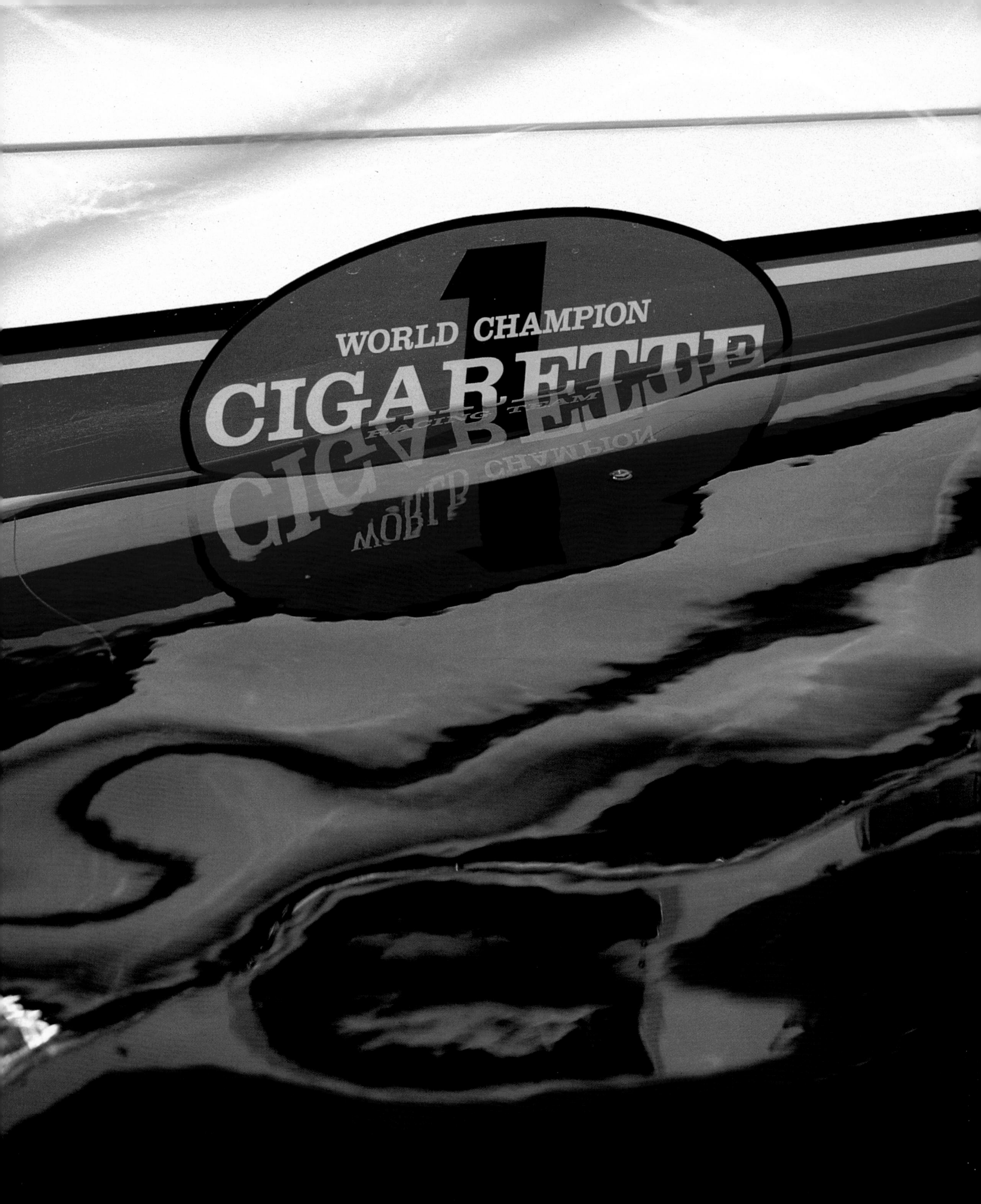
1
WORLD CHAMPION
CIGARETTE
RACING TEAM

boasts a shining light in the person of Henry Ford, the boating industry also features a leading man— Christopher Columbus Smith. Better known as Chris Smith, and founder of the Chris-Craft Corporation, this innovator began experimenting with gasoline-powered boats at the turn of the century.

By the outbreak of World War I, Smith, a driving force behind the rise of powerboat racing, was building boats capable of speeds in excess of 50 mph. In collaboration with Gar Wood, another pioneer racer and future boat builder, Smith went on to develop the first of the famous Miss Detroit gold-cup-winners.

Throughout the twenties and thirties, Gar Wood continued to extend the limits of speed and power, constructing and campaigning some of the most awesome machines ever to split the waves—the legendary Miss America racers. The last of these— and the first to shatter the 100 mph barrier—was powered by no less than four supercharged V-12 Packard airplane engines, developing 1,600 hp each.

Both racing and pleasure boat production came to a virtual standstill during World War II. Hydrodynamic advancements, however, in connection with the development of fast patrol boats for the military, as well as successful experiments with a revolutionary new material called GRP—glass-reinforced plastic—set the stage for explosive growth after the war.

Fiberglass turned out to be the perfect material for the construction of hulls, and the industry was quick to adapt. Only Chris-Craft—that champion of wooden mass production techniques—found it difficult to adjust, entering a period of financial uncertainty and internal upheaval.

On the previous page, a model of Don Aronow's 1969 Cigarette, the progenitor of the modern muscle boat. Here, a close-up of the Cigarette logo just above the waterline. Like the Ferrari emblem, this logo is a status symbol among pundits of exotic machinery.

It was in this climate of feverish competition that another man, one who would become the godfather of the modern muscle boat, made his flamboyant entry on the stage. Don Aronow was a real estate developer from New Jersey and he had made a fortune before the age of thirty. In 1960 he decided to retire at thirty-three. Moving to Florida, he soon found himself drawn to offshore racing—and the career that would bring him fame.

In Miami, Aronow made the acquaintance of men such as Dick Bertram and Jim Wynne, both experienced designers and racers. In Claudia—a wooden seventeen-footer designed by Wynne— Aronow made his first attempt at conquering the waves, finishing fourth in the 1962 Miami-Nassau race.

But outright victory was Aronow's ambition. He founded Formula Boat Company to facilitate his search for a design that would help him reach that goal. After months of experimentation Aronow launched the Formula 233, a twenty-three-footer designed by Wynne and Walt Walters. The fiberglass hull was shaped according to Ray Hunt's deep-vee principle, but the bow was more pointed and the entry sharper.

In 1963, Aronow ran the Miami-Nassau race in another deep-vee Formula—a twenty-seven-footer designed by Bertram and Peter Gurke. He finished third. He also started another trend by selling the boat following the race. Working with Wynne, Aronow then proceeded to design a new boat that became the first Donzi, a twenty-eight-footer. The year of 1965 finally brought him the long-coveted Miami-Nassau victory. Campaigning his Donzi, powered by a pair of 1,000 hp Holman-Moody Fords, he beat the rest of the field.

Aronow, always the restless entrepreneur, soon decided to sell Donzi, only to immediately start a new company, Magnum. In 1967, he began designing boats on his own, making them both longer and narrower. Behind the controls of the Maltese

Magnum—a single-engine twenty-seven-footer—he won both the US and the world offshore championships.

In 1968, Aronow sold Magnum and, true to form, soon fathered another design—this time it was the legendary Cigarette. He campaigned two of his new thirty-two-footers, powered by twin MerCruiser stern drives and producing close to 1,000 hp. Again he captured both championship titles. Also that year, Aronow built the thirty-five-foot Cigarette, a design hailed as the best deep-vee to date and a creation that became the model for the modern muscle boat.

A comprehensive review of the muscle boat as a broad concept should rightfully include a number of types—in particular, the wooden speedboats of the thirties, the hydroplane racers of the fifties and the California-style flat-bottom dragsters of today. But these will have to be relegated to future books. For now, the subject at hand is the offspring of the deep-vee hull—as raced and refined by Don Aronow, as built by some of the companies he founded and inspired, and as sleek and colorful images reflecting the glamorous beat of today's boating scene.

The launch of a 1978 vintage Cigarette racer, held aloft on a marina forklift.

Mahogany immortals combine muscle with old-world craftsmanship

A wooden classic projects elegance rather than brute power, and most mahogany runabouts certainly cannot match the formidable performance of the modern muscle boat. Still, there are some old-timers that pack powerful engines beneath that flawlessly varnished wood.

One of the most potent muscle boats of the fifties, Chris-Craft's finned Cobra in its optimal form with a 285 hp V-8 Cadillac, was capable of an impressive 55 mph. Built exclusively in 1955, the Cobra came in two sizes: a three-passenger eighteen-footer, of which only fifty-two were constructed; and a four-passenger twenty-one-footer, reproduced just fifty-six times.

While Chris-Craft was the undisputed champion among American boat manufacturers, the Italian firm Riva—dating back to 1869—could lay claim to the European title. Thanks to an emphasis on quality, Riva had enjoyed steady success but after World War II the firm found the going tough. The great grandson of the founder finally managed to establish a steady course, only to sell out to American interests in 1969.

Until then Riva built wooden boats exclusively. The new owners added fiberglass to the menu, launching a luxurious line of yachts while still continuing the classic models. The most prestigious of the wooden Rivas is the Super Aquarama. First offered in 1961, about 700 units have since been built.

The pair of classics featured on this and the following pages—an eighteen-foot Cobra and a 1964 Super Aquarama—form a nostalgic prologue to a look at the modern world of muscle boats.

It took Mike DaPron of Rossmoor, California, ten years to find a Cobra, and eight years to restore the bull-nosed beauty pictured on the previous page. The unique eighteen-footer, its shape inspired by the unlimited hydroplane racers of the era, was originally powered by a six-cylinder Hercules racing engine. It now sports a big-block Chevy, shown in the picture to the right. While the hull is built the old-fashioned way, with carefully selected mahogany, the engine cover and the for-looks-only fin—pictured in the close-up above— were manufactured from fiberglass, a first for Chris-Craft, which was slow to adopt modern manufacturing methods. Craftsmanship, on the other hand, was always at a premium. This was reflected by the fact that it took 263 hours of labor to fashion the hull of the Cobra, and by the price, which ranged from $3,710 for the eighteen-footer to $6,560 for the twenty-one-footer. A Cadillac Eldorado, by comparison, cost $6,286 in 1955. Today, the Cobra has become one of the most collectible of classic muscle boats.

Scott DaPron, a collector of anything that moves fast and looks good, bought his 1964 Riva Super Aquarama from an enthusiast in Sweden. The original owner had kept the boat on the French Riviera, the traditional playground for classic Rivas. To the left, DaPron, of Lake Arrowhead, California, ponders the automobile-style dash of his mahogany masterpiece. The instrument cluster features twin tachometers mounted immediately ahead of the steering wheel, registering the speed of each of the engines independently. Shifting is activated via the column-mounted lever, and the twin throttles are located on the dash; in this scene, the assembly is obscured by DaPron's left hand. On the following page, the Riva's sleek twenty-seven-foot exterior. Carlo Riva, having taken over the helm of the company in the early fifties, made his mark by developing a new process called "armored lamination," which helped alleviate some of the problems plaguing wooden boats as a result of contraction and expansion.

When the first Aquaramas went on sale in the United States in 1964, prospective buyers—when opening those luxuriously padded hatches—were pleasantly surprised to find the same engines that were under the hoods of their Chevrolet Corvettes, rather than some mysteriously exotic machinery from an Italian low-volume builder. But this was perfectly in line with Riva tradition; from the beginning, the company had been using American-supplied powerplants such as Chris-Craft, Gray and, later, Chrysler. Pictured to the left, owner DaPron checks the oil before taking off on a tour of Lake Perris. His Riva still features the original 327 ci, 300 hp GM engines. Having found them low on power and ready for extensive overhaul, DaPron plans to fit modern high-performance replacements. Pictured above, the trappings of traditional elegance. The fittings are all made from brass, and chromed in Riva's own facility. The fact that these particular items still feature the original finish is ample proof of the famous Riva quality.

USA Racing Team: Staying on the course staked out by the master

In spite of the name, USA Racing Team is not an active competition organization—although it could have been.

At the time of his premature death in 1987, Don Aronow—the firm's famous founder—had been concentrating the collected wisdom of his career as a builder and campaigner of offshore raceboats into one single project, a new hull. And, in order to prove the validity of the design, he had decided to return to the circuit after a fifteen-year absence.

When Aronow sold his Cigarette organization, he was prohibited from building a similar product for a stipulated period of time. The boats he conceived for the manufacturing program of his USA Racing Team were therefore of a twin-hull configuration. Two basic designs—and three sizes—were available: thirty-nine- and twenty-seven-foot Catamarans, which are actually deep-vees split in two; and the twenty-four-foot Relentless, a true catamaran.

Although Aronow's racing plans will never be realized—at least not with him at the wheel—his legacy lives on through the hull he created. The slim beauty, whose basic shape Aronow had built with his own hands, sat unattended at the plant for almost a year, as the creator's sudden death caused an understandable paralysis within the firm. But during the spring of 1988—with the blessing and support of Aronow's son—finishing touches were applied.

At this time, the first completed hull is anticipated. The sentiment is that this design, like so many of Aronow's previous ones, will also become a milestone.

The picture on the previous page captures Don Aronow's last effort—his forty-five-foot racing hull—and marks the first time it was photographed for the public. The final sanding of the plug is being completed here. The plug is the actual body to be used in making the boat's mold, inside of which all future hulls will be formed. The picture to the right illustrates the super-narrow shape of the design—just eight feet wide, the width of an average thirty-footer. Power is to come from three inboard engines, mounted in a staggered fashion. Pictured above is Don Aronow's son Michael. After his father's death he vowed to finish the project. In 1967, at the age of seventeen, young Aronow began crewing with the team, and in 1969 became a permanent member—thus finishing one of the most glorious seasons ever recorded in the annals of offshore racing. An automobile accident in 1970 left him in a wheel-chair—yet still filled with his father's famous fighting spirit.

The twenty-four-foot Relentless—a below-the-waterline view of its twin-hull is seen in the photograph on the previous page—has an eight-foot beam and weighs 3,400 lb. Width of the tunnel between the hulls is just under four feet. Above, production manager Ralph Johnson, who worked with Don Aronow since the days of the Cigarette, takes the sleek prototype for a test drive in the canal near the USA Racing Team's factory. Standard power comes from twin outboards: V-6 Mercurys, each producing 260 hp. The top speed is an impressive 100 mph. The price tag for such speed is a relatively reasonable $60,000. The twin-hull design and the resulting shallow depth require the crew to sit while in action—a mode facilitated by the tight-hugging chairs, seen to the right. A complete set of instruments are mounted on the dash and on a console between the seats. A bench seat, placed behind the driver and the front passenger, allows room for three additional passengers.

Captured here is the nerve center of
USA Racing Team's largest
production boat, the thirty-nine-foot
Catamaran. The layout is pure racing,
following the design developed by
Aronow during his many years of
offshore racing. The configuration
calls for a crew of three, positioned
side by side. The throttler—if right-
handed—occupies a place on the right.
The driver, attending to the steering
wheel, is situated in the middle. The
navigator is located on the left. All are
supported in their stand-up positions
by amply padded bolsters. The
bolsters are of vital importance: the
crew must be able to withstand
shocks, measured by G-force meters,
that produce more than twice the
force endured by astronauts on
takeoff. The "civilian" Catamaran is
set up for one-person operation, and
features Morse-manufactured controls
that combine shifting and throttle
operation in the same unit.

30

Featured here, the Blue Thunder, US Customs' version of the USA Racing Team thirty-nine-foot Catamaran. The agency made the choice after careful testing and consideration of the outstanding handling capabilities of the Catamaran. Thanks to its deep-vee configuration and its wide beam—nearly twelve feet—the Catamaran is so stable it can execute a 360 degree turn in its own wake at top speed, said to be more than 70 mph. To date, forty-two units have been built, Customs' Blue Thunders included. On the previous page, the engine package

hidden below the hydraulically operated twin hatches: two 575 MerCruiser stern drives—modified 540 ci big-block Chevys, producing 575 hp—topped off by Stelling headers, a custom exhaust system and MerCruiser Speedmaster III drives. All this for a mere $239,000. Of course, if a prospective buyer can spare that much money, he or she surely ought to spring for a custom trailer as well—just $9,500. And why not a spare set of Speedmaster props? A mere $3,000.

The twenty-million-dollar treasure of Fort Apache Marina

If Miami is the boating capital of the world, then 188th Street in North Miami Beach must certainly be one of its main thoroughfares. Between the dark-watered twin canals of this dead-end street hides a sprawling center of activity, a hotspot where sleek-bodied muscle boats are designed and built, launched and tested, stored and merchandized—a mecca for admirers of fast and furious machinery of the floating kind.

Just as the deep-vee muscle boat—as a product and as a phenomenon—was popularized by Don Aronow, the concentration of activity to 188th Street must also be attributed to this larger-than-life figure. It was here that Aronow built his first Formula boats—the facilities are still in use today. It was also here that he founded his Cigarette organization—also still in place, occupying buildings on both sides of the street. And it was here that he located the last of his boating ventures, the USA Racing Team.

The drab facades and cluttered yards of the manufacturing plants do not provide the most exciting color of this spot; that distinction belongs to Fort Apache Marina. In a space no larger than a few acres, $20 million worth of muscle boats are stored within the bowels of three four-story high-rises. Launch and service facilities, mooring docks—as well as a canal-side restaurant and bar—complete the trendy setup.

The angled drives and the suspended outboards protruding precariously from the rows of transoms—many-colored and multi-shaped—form an attractive pattern and a fascinating map to muscle boat country.

The scene featured on the opening pages of this chapter captures the early morning stillness at Fort Apache Marina; soon this hotspot of South Florida muscle boat activity will be buzzing with business. Already in the water, a Cigarette Top Gun lies ready and able to take on the day's chores. On the quay, not yet launched, can be seen the sweeping silhouette of a Fountain muscle boat. The yacht-style bow of this North Carolina-built craft makes it easy to spot. On the previous page, a view of one of the four storage buildings that make up the core of this state-of-the-art facility. To the left, one of the two specially equipped forklifts operating at the marina reaches sixty feet in the air to catch a Donzi. Above, a Scarab has just been lowered into the launching dock. On the following page, the time has come to launch a USA Racing Team Catamaran. Even this 9,000 lb. hunk is no match for the heavy-duty machinery.

Cigarette Racing Team: Thoroughbreds with magical appeal

There is a striking parallel between Ferrari, the legendary marque among exotic sports cars, and Cigarette, the image leader among exotic muscle boats. The founder of the Italian thoroughbred, Enzo Ferrari, built only competition machines in the beginning, as winning races was his sole objective. Later, in order to fund his costly obsession, Ferrari began building limited numbers of street machines.

After Don Aronow's retirement from competition, the founder of Cigarette continued to produce raceboats. His creations crossed the finish line as winners of seven world and twenty US titles. With successes like these to vouch for the excellence of the design, the step to building boats for the general market was a natural one. Later, displaying his well-known restlessness, he sold Cigarette, then bought it back, only to sell it again. In 1984, when Jeff Friedman became the new owner, production had reached sixty units per year.

Seeing a potential for deeper market penetration, Friedman hired Bob Gowens, a management consultant with experience from the world of corporate giants, to run his new acquisition. A thorough restructuring of the manufacturing and marketing aspects of the business resulted in today's streamlined Cigarette organization.

An increase in production to around 150 units per year did not compromise the appeal of the product. Nor did commercialization cause a cutting of the ties to racing; in 1986, Craig Barrie, the firm's dynamic marketing director, managed to bring home the prestigious Gold Coast Cup.

Captured on the previous page while skimming the inviting waters of Florida's Intracoastal Waterway, is Cigarette's top performer, the thirty-eight-foot Top Gun—molded directly from Cigarette's famous US and world championship winner. Owner Greg Chu of New York is at the helm of his pride and joy, which he bought off the floor of the 1987 New York Boat Show. His was the first Top Gun to be equipped with the 420 MerCruiser setup. To the left, a Cafe Racer—Cigarette's thirty-five-footer—traverses the turbulent waters of Miami Beach's Haulover Gap. Above, Buddy Currier, Cigarette's chief mechanic, revs up a Bullet—the company's latest creation, a thirty-one-footer—heading out of the canal flowing in front of the Cigarette plant in North Miami Beach. Currier's assistant stands ready with the radar gun. On the following page, the Cigarette test team puts a Cafe Racer through its paces. If it doesn't do at least 66 mph, something is wrong and it goes right back to the shop.

To the right, a bird's-eye view illustrates the layout of a Cigarette Top Gun. Twin racing-style bolsters, with a removable unit for a third spot plus a rear bench seat, provides room for six to seven occupants. Under the deck, with its flush, racing-style hatches, is a roomy cabin with a fully enclosed head. Behind the cockpit sprawls the engine hatch, hydraulically operated and covered with a sun pad. And beneath the hatch hides the heart of the matter—or, rather, the twin hearts. Power ranges from twin 420 MerCruisers to twin 572 Hawks, the latter equipped with Speedmaster III drives. Prices for the boats range from $160,000 to $260,000. Included in the highest-priced package is a hull manufactured from Kevlar laminate. This is the latest in boat-building technology and saves weight, a crucial factor for increased speed. The Kevlar hull is also stronger, of vital importance when performance is up. Above, a close-up of the Top Gun cockpit, from which all the firepower is triggered.

The thirty-one-foot Bullet is Cigarette's newest contribution to the rapidly expanding population of the muscle boat world. And this craft is a true styling trend-setter—a point underscored by *Boating* magazine, which included it in its list of the ten best boats of 1987. Featured here, the Bullet's helm station. In order to perpetuate the long-hooded look, a feature easily lost when the overall length is cut down, the Cigarette design team created an instrument panel with a sharper incline, leaving much of the behind-the-scenes gear pushed forward under the fairing. In addition to Kiekhaefer throttle and shift control, Ritchie compass, and Gaffrig speedometer, the panel features complete Stewart Warner instrumentation with a leather-covered steering wheel. Speaking of leather, the cabin can be upholstered with the real thing—a $3,500 option, for which one gets the look and the smell of a classic Rolls-Royce. As a base package, fitted with twin MerCruisers and Bravo drives, the Bullet lists at $110,000.

Provided the buyer can show a pocketbook fat enough to pay the price, there is no limit to the way a Cigarette can be rigged. The photograph above shows an engine option not found in the official price list: the Keith-Hazel version of Chevy's venerable big-block favorite, the pair producing a combined horsepower figure of 1,300 and a top speed of more than 90 mph. To the right, the basic MerCruiser engine setup, complete with gleaming stainless steel through-transom open exhaust pipes for maximum performance and perfect exhaust note, the metallic roar that makes the competition shudder miles away. At the moment this photo was shot, the engines had just been shut off and a trickle of the flow-through seawater used for cooling, still drips from the pipes. On the following page, the top-of-the-line drive setup, the Speedmaster III unit, complete with torpedo-shaped crescent lowers. Here, the drives are tilted to their most upright position.

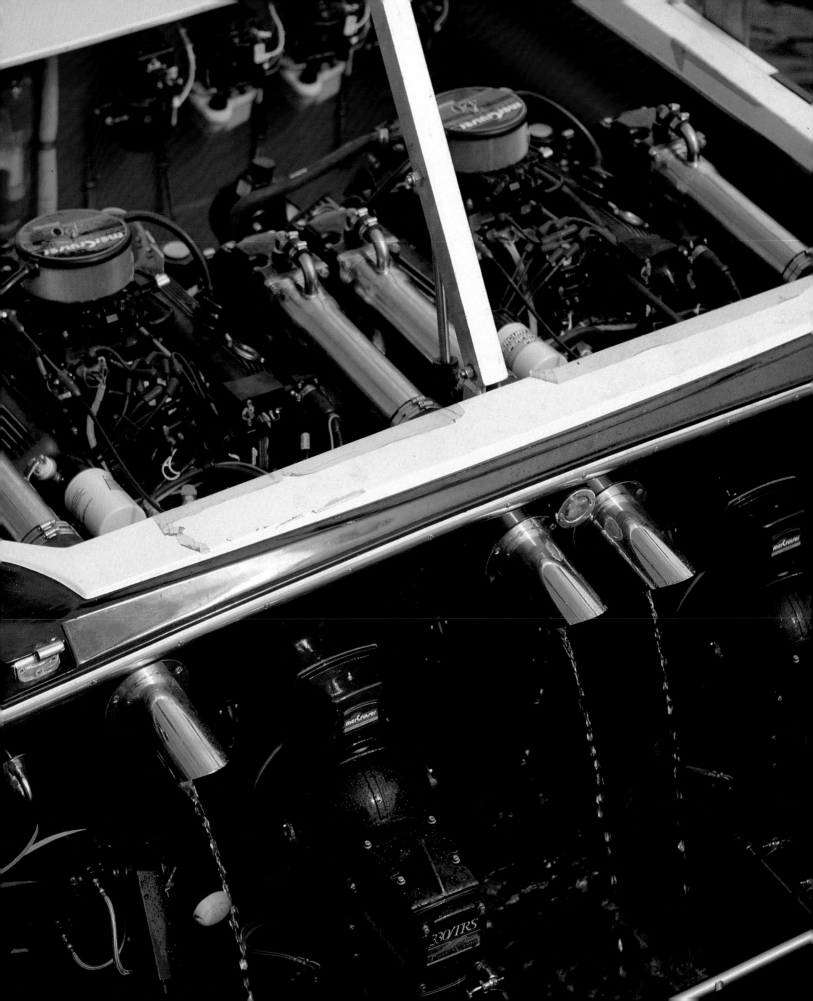

Where the clientele is rich and famous, the boats rakish and fast

In the fifties it was neon-decorated Mel's Diner in Hollywood and cruising on Main Street. Operative names were Corvette and Eldorado and Turnpike Cruiser. In the sixties it was Detroit's Woodward Avenue and life-and-death duels on the back road dragstrip. Names that made the pulse run quicker were Barracuda and Firebird and Mustang.

In today's world of muscle boats it is Shooters bar and restaurant. The site is convenient and intriguing, hugging the water's edge along the Intracoastal Waterway in Florida's posh Fort Lauderdale. Names that make heads turn are Cigarette and Scarab and Formula.

Shooters is shaded by palms, with a well-stocked bar and gourmet food on the menu. The restaurant reverberates with the rumbling of muscle boat engines, the gurgling of propeller turbulence and the slapping of waves against slick hulls from the other boats' wakes. The air is spiced with the aroma of the ocean and tanning lotions. All in all, Shooters concocts a mix that has turned it into a hotspot for muscle boat enthusiasts and a gold mine for the owners of the establishment; Shooters has become the thirteenth largest-grossing restaurant in the nation.

A steady stream of boats floats past the restaurant. No matter whether the boats' occupants are taking in the scenery, waiting for a mooring spot or simply showing off, the parade makes for a fascinating view of muscle machinery. Perhaps the setting is somewhat over-indulgent—but that is, after all, what today's life in the fast lane is all about.

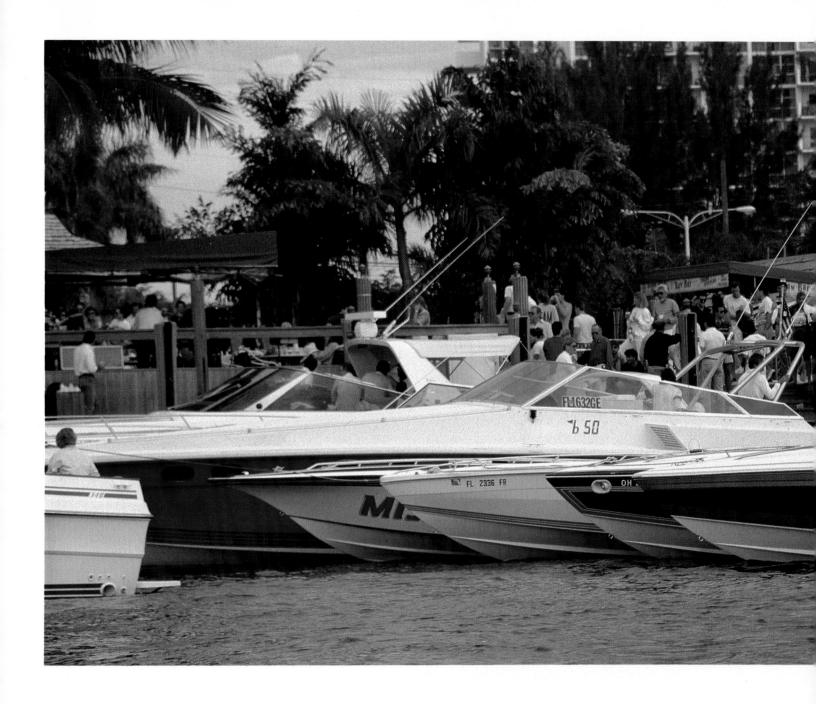

On the previous page, framed by the lazy palms at Shooters and turning slowly in the mild current of the Intracoastal Waterway, a Cougar Catamaran lounges in the middle of the traffic lane. Above, in a photograph shot from the Waterway, the same scene is captured from the vantage point of the Catamaran; in the background, lush tropical vegetation and the pastel-colored condominium high-rises of Fort Lauderdale. Weekend action at Shooters leaves the muscle boats stacked seven deep and yes, valet parking is available. The boat occupying the spot nearest to the camera is a Formula. Farther back in the line-up, a Fountain projects its stylistic bow. On the following page, the wide-angle lens records the traffic jam of muscle boats. The Waterway is quite narrow at this point and the rules of the no-wake zone are strictly enforced. The small boat approaching in the distance is a Donzi Classic.

Slipping silently past Shooters, above, is a thirty-one-foot Formula 311 SR-1—silently, because the Formula is equipped with a system called Silent Thunder. The transom platform is hollow and engine exhaust, mixed with cooling water, is routed into the cavity where a baffle divides the space into two chambers; the exhaust has to pass through the water and under the baffle to escape. Chris-Craft's Stinger, to the right, also features a transom landing, but in this case the space functions purely as a swim platform, although some degree of sound muffling is achieved thanks to the exhaust pipes exiting below the platform. Chris-Craft uses both OMC and MerCruiser power. The Stingers are available in a variety of sizes, ranging from a twenty-footer to a forty-one-footer, with the largest fetching a price near $140,000. The Chris-Craft sportboats are built in Bellingham, Washington; Bradenton, Florida; and Goshen, Indiana. Total annual production reaches about 750 units.

Donzi Marine: Understated elegance creates ultimate status symbol

The Donzi is yet another of Don Aronow's offspring. According to legend, the Donzi appellation was derived from the nickname given to Aronow by aviation pioneer Tommy Sopwith.

Founded in 1963, the company was later sold to Teleflex. Today Donzi is owned by industralist Dick Genth, himself a former offshore racer, whose resume boasts highly regarded stints at the helm of giants such as Thunderbird, Wellcraft and Chris-Craft.

Through the years, the mainstay of Donzi's product line has been the Classic Series. The models include the 18, a 2,600 lb. eighteen-footer, powered by a single 270 hp MerCruiser; the Minx, a twenty-footer, powered as the 18, but weighing 100 pounds more; and the 22, a 3,300 lb. twenty-two-footer, powered by a 330 hp V-8. All the boats are based on designs by Walt Walters and all display a grace and simplicity that underscores their link to the classic era.

When Genth took over in 1985, he hired Don Westerman to engineer a new line—the Z series, available in four sizes: twenty-one, twenty-five, twenty-nine and thirty-three feet.

Thanks to its understated elegance coupled with an uncompromising allegiance to quality, Donzis have become the favorite of muscle boat enthusiasts with discriminating taste. In 1988 a new volume-produced line—the Ragazza—was added. With factory space at a premium, the Classic and Z series were limited to an annual output of 500 units—a move that made the Donzis even more elitist.

The two previous photographs constitute ample proof that there indeed exists something called "poetry in motion." Both pictures feature Donzi's magnificent styling masterpiece—the Z-33 Crossbow—in action, first leaning deep during a turn, then shooting by at a top speed of around 70 mph. At the controls are factory test drivers Greg Bogart and Rick Brenner. First appearing at the Chicago Boat Show in 1985, the Z-33—together with its smaller cousins, the Z-21, the Z-25 and the Z-29—caused a sensation. Pictured here, an early Z boat. The unique burgundy color was used only on a few examples since it did not appeal to many buyers, who instead opted for flashier shades. And flash is what the present line offers, in four bright shades: yellow, red, teal and blue. The following photograph captures a 1988 Z-33 in all its sleek splendor. But such beauty does not come cheap. The price tag for a Z-33 equipped with 330 TRS MerCruisers is around $175,000.

Donzi's trend-setting emphasis on styling originates with Dick Genth, but the hands-on creativity is the responsibility of Dave Riley, pictured to the right, looking out from one of the Z-33's twin gullwing hatches. Above, the Donzi name contrasts decoratively with an intriguing row of "gills" which funnel oxygen to a hungry pair of engines. On the following page, a wide-angle view of the Z-33's cockpit, where Riley's attention to detail has paid off handsomely. The side-by-side driver/passenger seat assembly adjusts electrically. The dash is fully equipped and styled with round edges and organic shapes. The view is complemented by the smoothly curved plexiglass windshield, which has a curled upper lip to deflect the slipstream. Below deck, the combination of style and function continues with such amenities as a leather-upholstered jumpseat and a convertible dinette table. The four oval windows, together with the two large hatches, eliminate the closed-in feeling experienced in many other boats of this type.

The name of the game is flashing from the flanks

A boat must have a name. No question about it. The christening practice has been a tradition since time immemorial, and anyone having encountered a boat without a name will surely recall feeling that the craft was partly naked and unfinished.

The ancient christening custom called for the boat to be designated after a beloved female. A stroll along the beaches of a Spanish fishing village still provides evidence of this tradition, revealing rows of artfully decorated hulls, proudly displaying on their curved bows the names of mothers and saints and girlfriends.

Today, the tradition of christening has not changed. What has changed are the themes of the names—especially as they pertain to the muscle boat. The expressions are now clever, quick and catchy, often balancing on the edge of outrageous. And they are often as far from the past as today's lifestyle of lost innocence is from the quaintness of yesteryear.

The name of the game is now more than ever a reflection of the ego—the ability, the success, the boldness of the owner. And although there are still to be seen the congenial "I Love My Wife" and "Me and My Lady," it is appellations such as "The Devil In Me" and "On The Cutting Edge" that attract admiring attention.

There is a splash of Catch-22 in a name like "Lethal Weapon," as seen here. Once the epithet is painted on the side, it cries out for the boat to be handled with all the audacity implied.

Much of the visual appeal of the muscle boat stems from the designs applied to their sleek bodies, usually executed with flowing stripes and glowing colors. The price lists of some manufacturers include the cost of basic paint jobs. A simple two-tone color scheme, for instance, might add just $500 to the total. The fancier the design, the higher the cost. Cigarette charges $2,000, $2,500 and $3,000 for the Trophy, the Competitor and the Champion, respectively—three categories of standardized graphics.

Custom designs are quoted on an individual basis. Featured here are two schools of thought. Above, a Cigarette Top Gun, finished for a Florida customer, sports a triple-tone paint scheme and a flavorful name with double meaning. To the right, another Cigarette, executed for delivery to a customer on the French Riviera, exemplifies a decidedly decorous approach, featuring the classic traveler's salutation, equivalent to our "God's Speed."

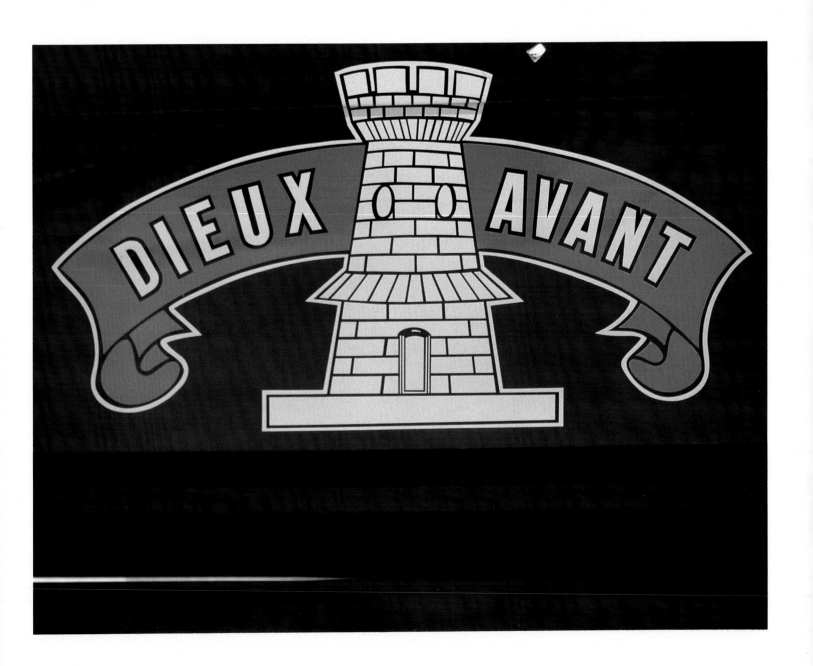

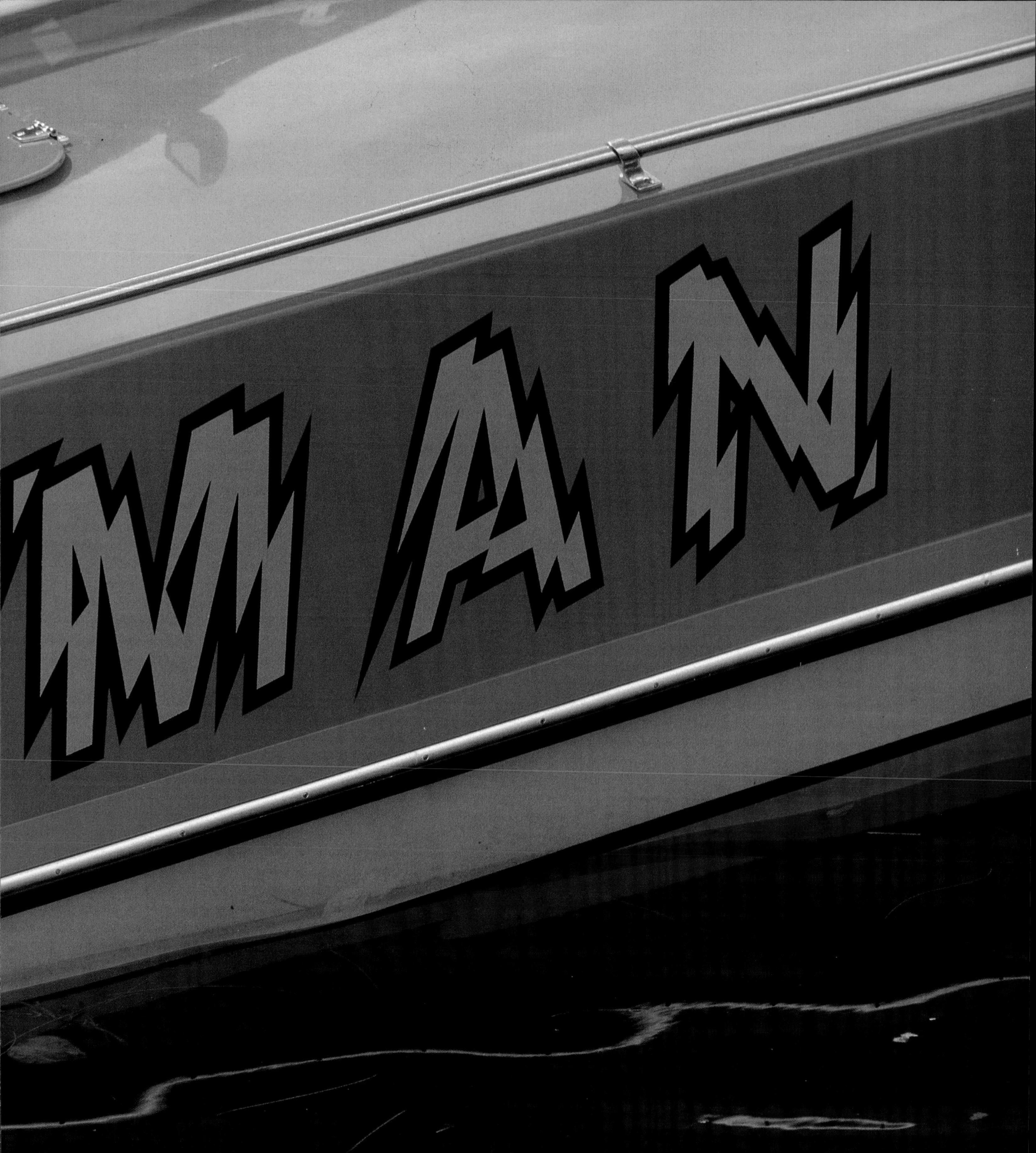
MAN

The basic color of a boat is applied before the hull is built—as a first step in the lay-up process, a thick layer of gelcoat is sprayed onto the surface of the mold. The materials used for the actual structure—the resin and the matting—are then added. When completed, the gelcoat forms the final surface—no other finish is needed. But most owners want a fancy look, for which Imron is used—a heavy-duty paint, originally developed for the aircraft industry. Lettering and

graphics are applied with adhesive foils. The owner of a boat is able to polish the surface for the ultimate sheen, using standard automotive products. The previous photograph features the name chosen by the owner of a Cougar Catamaran. The blurring of the letters may have been an effort to illustrate the bone-jarring sensation experienced during a high-speed ride in such a craft. Above, the use of silver foil gives a decorative mirror effect.

84

Tempest Marine:
Making waves
with ideas that work

Dick Simon is a businessman and boating enthusiast with a specific demand—he wants things to work. Originally from Chicago, Simon tired of the harsh winters and moved to Florida. He celebrated a new lifestyle by exploring the virtues of a series of sportboats and yachts.

Finding himself in need of a particular type of craft that was both fast and reliable, he ordered such a design from a small builder. Unsatisfied, he ended up buying the company. Thus, in the summer of 1982, began a new era at Tempest Marine.

With Simon providing the impetus in the form of capital and direction, one important ingredient in the recipe for success was present. The other ingredient in the form of a brilliant designer with fresh ideas was harder to come by—until destiny steered Adam Erdberg onto an intersecting course with Simon.

An Israeli, Erdberg holds an engineering degree from Technion Institute of Technology in Haifa. Arriving in Florida in 1974, he first worked on the Bertram assembly line. From there he soon moved to the design office, and later opened his own consulting firm. During that period, Erdberg was responsible for the design of Cigarette's forty-one-footer.

Today, a Cigarette neighbor on North Miami Beach's 188th Street, Erdberg can take credit for a series of winners, among them Tempest's forty-four-footer. Powered by twin Caterpillar engines and equipped with Erdberg's patented T-Torque surface drive, this relentless performer was selected by the US Coast Guard to become its Fast Coast Interceptor—FCI—to be used for tough drug enforcement work.

For a small company, Tempest Marine offers an incredible range of designs. The complete list of hulls includes lengths of thirty-two, thirty-eight, forty-two, forty-four, sixty and eighty-five feet. The two latter hulls were conceived for a new line of high-performance yachts. The hottest of the muscle boats is the new thirty-two-footer, available with stern drive as the Sport and with outboards as the Europa. The thirty-two-foot configuration allows for the ultimate combination of weight, for maximum performance, and size, for maneuverability without loss of offshore handling characteristics. A Sport is seen in action on the previous page. Here, the rear exhausts of the Tempest. On the following page, one of the Tempest-built Coast Guard FCIs, pictured in offshore action. For the ultimate in reliability, these boats are powered by two V-12 Caterpillars. The turbocharged, aftercooled diesels produce 1,000 hp at 2,100 rpm, for a top speed of more than 60 mph.

Design and technology at Tempest is state of the art. To the left, the racy frontal aspect of the Sport, sculpted under the direction of Adam Erdberg, whose past experience includes creating high-speed patrol boats for the Israeli navy. Nothing is compromised when it comes to materials and workmanship—the lifting strakes, for instance, are filled with micro-balloon foam, then covered with layers of mat and roving. The result is the maximum in hull rigidity. If anything is lacking, it is frills; the Sport is strictly for business,

like an all-out sports car. Above, Erdberg explains his T-Torque, a revolutionary drive system he invented when no other available product would do. On the following page, a side view of the Sport's knife-like bow. In the background, the actual mold from which each hull originates. Unlike many deep-vees marketed today, the Sport is not a copy-cat design. Erdberg added one digit to the classic twenty-four-degree dead rise of the Ray Hunt original. The result was an improved offshore ride.

The Europa is powered by outboard engines—an increasingly viable alternative which not only leaves more cockpit room but also is less costly. Furthermore, there is space to mount multiple units. In some cases as many as four have been lined up behind the transom; if one goes out, there are three left. But there are drawbacks: since outboard engines work on the two-cycle principle, there are smoke and odor to contend with. And, perhaps more devastating to some, there is the lack of that macho roar so typical of big four-cycle inboards—although to others the high-pitched whine from multiple two-strokers is just as exhilarating. The boat featured here—destined for Hong Kong delivery—is powered by two Johnson counter-rotating V-8s. Producing 300 hp each, they are now the most powerful on the market. Thus equipped, the Europa runs about $100,000. The Sport, fitted with twin 420 MerCruiser TRS stern drives, will set the buyer back another $25,000.

96

Tempest's Super Sport is sure to turn heads. The boat features a pair of Porsche's recently developed marine engines. New York-based Titanium Marine, which holds the marketing rights, selected Tempest's thirty-two-footer for the ground-breaking effort based on its outstanding hull characteristics. The eye-catching machine idling along in a no-wake zone of the Intracoastal Waterway—as seen on the previous page—is the prototype. Pictured on these pages, the deck section of the second unit. Future hulls will be made from Kevlar laminate. This material, coupled with the lightweight Porsche engines, will shave about 1,500 pounds off the 6,500 lb. standard Sport version. On the following page, the Sport and the Super Sport are shown moored side by side. Performance in the form of raw power is not the primary objective. Rather, performance in the form of reliability and longevity is the goal. Porsche calls for maintenance intervals of 500 hours—a point at which most other high-performance machines have already given their best.

The spoiler is not just an attention-grabber. It also applies downforce to the aft of the boat, an important aspect since the Porsche engines are lighter than the units the hull was originally designed for. The spoiler is attached to the hydraulically operated hatch, which, instead of a sun pad, features two plexiglass windows appropriately decorated with Porsche emblems. The Porsche engineers began with the proven 928 sports car V-8—complete with its four-valve-head design, its Jetronic fuel injection and its EZF ignition system teaming up to yield 320 hp at 6,000 rpm. Added was a special triple-circulation cooling system. The first closed circulation route cools the block. The second, also closed, cools the manifolds. The third route is open—driven by a seawater pump—and cools the exchanger tubes and the exhaust system. For the enthusiast with racing performance on the wish list, there is a twin-turbocharged version producing as much as 750 hp at 6,700 rpm. The Tempest Porsche Super Sport, in its basic form, carries a neat little price tag of $175,000.

The popularity of the muscle boat penetrates the marketplace

In 1987 Americans spent $14 billion on boats, related equipment and services—more than on such essentials as cosmetics, dog food and rock music. While the muscle boat is by no means the main share of this booming market, its popularity is growing rapidly.

No small measure of the success of the muscle boat can be attributed to the image-building effect of such visual acrobatics as performed every week in the title segment of television's *Miami Vice,* whose main character, Don Johnson—not coincidentally—has become involved with racing. As a driver, the star was a part of the three-man Wellcraft Scarab team that emerged as the winners of the grueling 1987 Mississippi River Race.

While originally a domain of small, exclusive builders—pioneered by Aronow—now, with the booming demand for muscle boats, even the huge, mass-production-oriented manufacturers have jumped aboard, moves exemplified by a host of pseudo-muscle boats.

And while the heart of the muscle boat business is still centered in Miami, manufacturers all over the country—from Baja in Ohio, to Carrera in Michigan, to Eliminator in California—are competing for places in the sunshine.

On the following pages, a camera tour along the mooring docks and waterways of southern Florida affords glimpses of some of the machines vying for attention in the wake of the soaring popularity of the breed.

On the opening page of the chapter, a Chris-Craft catamaran. On the previous page, an example of one of the modern-era muscle boat pioneers, the Scarab. The original Scarab was conceived by Californian Larry Smith, a designer, builder and racer, who—much like Don Aronow—proved his product on the offshore circuit. In 1974, Smith sold Scarab to Wellcraft—the third largest boat manufacturer in the nation, located in Sarasota. The Scarab line of muscle boats spans the spectrum of sizes, from the smallest, the twenty-six-foot Nova Spyder—costing just under $50,000 when equipped with twin 260 MerCruisers—to the brand new fifty-foot Meteor 5000—a luxurious high-performance boat powered by triple 420 MerCruisers. Also new is the Don Johnson Signature edition—a forty-three-footer patterned on the boat the star drove to victory in the St. Louis to New Orleans race. The ultimate in performance and luxury, this craft is powered by 685 MerCruiser Lamborghinis, and carries a price tag of $350,000. To the left, the cockpit of Scarab's thirty-eight-footer, and above, its potent power—two 575 MerCruisers.

Pictured to the left and on the previous page, a thirty-two-foot Midnight Express Sport, manufactured by a company with the same provocative name located in Opa-Locka, Florida. This boat builder, like so many others, grew out of the Aronow nucleus. Founder Byng Good worked alongside Aronow for a number of years before setting up his own company in 1979. Available with outboard or inboard power and built in thirty-two-, thirty-seven- and forty-seven-foot versions, annual production is approximately fifty units. Above,

the roomy engine compartment of a Cougar equipped with 575 MerCruisers. Two fuel tanks, one on each side, hold a combined total of 340 gallons. At full throttle this supply will last for about five hours. Anyone having experienced even just fifteen minutes of full-throttle action knows that 70 or 80 mph on the water in no way compares to the same speed on the asphalt. In other words, only racers and folks with a guilty conscience run at full throttle for any longer period of time.

Pictured here, the thirty-eight-foot Cougar, heralded as one of the most advanced boats on the market—and certainly one of the most expensive. The styling is unique, with its upswept fairing and its raised, wing-like rear deck. Built in Hamble, Hampshire, England, the Cougar organization was instrumental in developing the catamaran concept for offshore racing. Founder Ted Toleman proved the soundness of the design by capturing numerous championship titles. Cougar markets three catamarans—twenty-five-, twenty-seven- and thirty-footers. The vee bottoms also come in a threesome— thirty-three-, thirty-eight- and forty-six-footers. The thirty-eight-footer— its state-of-the-art cockpit shown on the following page—costs $325,000. It is powered by 575 MerCruisers and driven by top-of-the-line Speedmaster IVs. Thus outfitted, maximum speed is reportedly in the 90 mph range. The forty-six-footer represents a further expansion in both comfort features and price—a cool half a million dollars buys a fully equipped example of Cougar's fabulous flagship.

A converted racer is as close as one can get to the real thing and still call it a pleasure boat. The awesome-looking contraption seen here is another version of the English-built Cougar. Conceived in 1982 for serious use on the offshore racing circuit, this particular example was one of the company's earliest catamarans. But the boat did not fulfill the high hopes of its designers, and when subsequent versions made it obsolete, the prototype was relegated to a life of relative leisure. Originally powered by inboard engines and propelled by Arneson drives, it now sports four 3.4 EFI Mercury V-6 outboards, which boast a combined output of 1,240 hp. Powered by this setup, close to 90 mph has been recorded by its driver and caretaker, Bob Baranowski, of Robert's Marine Service in Pembroke Park, Florida. The flared spoilers are just for show. Under the cockpit canopy sits four Recaro seats, modified with enlarged lateral support wings that help keep the occupants in place.

Featured here, the Sonic 36 SS, a boat expressly for folks who want to go fast. This unit sports a Mediterranean mast—basically a looks-only item as far as aerodynamics is concerned—but put to good use as the foundation for radar equipment, spotlights and speakers. The Sonic was conceived by Jay Ross, who began tinkering with boats as a thirteen-year-old. Bitten by the bug, he grew up to build a string of boats for his own use, but demand from friends and acquaintances soon put him in the boat-manufacturing business. Today, with a new factory in Hollywood, Florida, Ross directs a company that produces approximately sixty boats each year and has a six-month backlog of orders. Rigged with 575 MerCruisers and Speedmaster IIIs, the 36 SS will do 85 mph and costs $225,000. The bottom-of-the-line thirty-footer, fitted with the MerCruiser Bravo setup, will run at 70 mph and cost $80,000. The luxurious top-of-the-line forty-one-footer, sporting 575 MerCruisers, as well as a cabin fortified with television, VCR, microwave oven and other goodies, will run at 78 mph and cost $250,000.

This close-up is of the power behind
the 90 mph top speed of the particular
Sonic shown on the previous pages—a
pair of super-potent Ferrara-tuned
Chevys, producing 650 hp each.
Dennis Ferrara, a former drag racing
champion, now president of Ferrara
Performance Engines in
Ronkonkoma, New York, offers a line
of some of the most outrageously
powerful machines in the business.
The standard line features a 585 hp,
650 hp and 745 hp range—with the
650 hp carrying a price tag of around
$15,000 per unit. There is also a high-
performance line—based on an all-
aluminum Chevy block—consisting of
three variations, a 780 hp, 825 hp and
900 hp. The 900 hp will set the buyer
back as much as $42,000. (A 1,000
hp concept engine has been rumored
to be running in the test facility.)
While most high-performance engines
demand high-octane fuel, Ferrara
insists on providing engines that run
on gas straight from the pump.

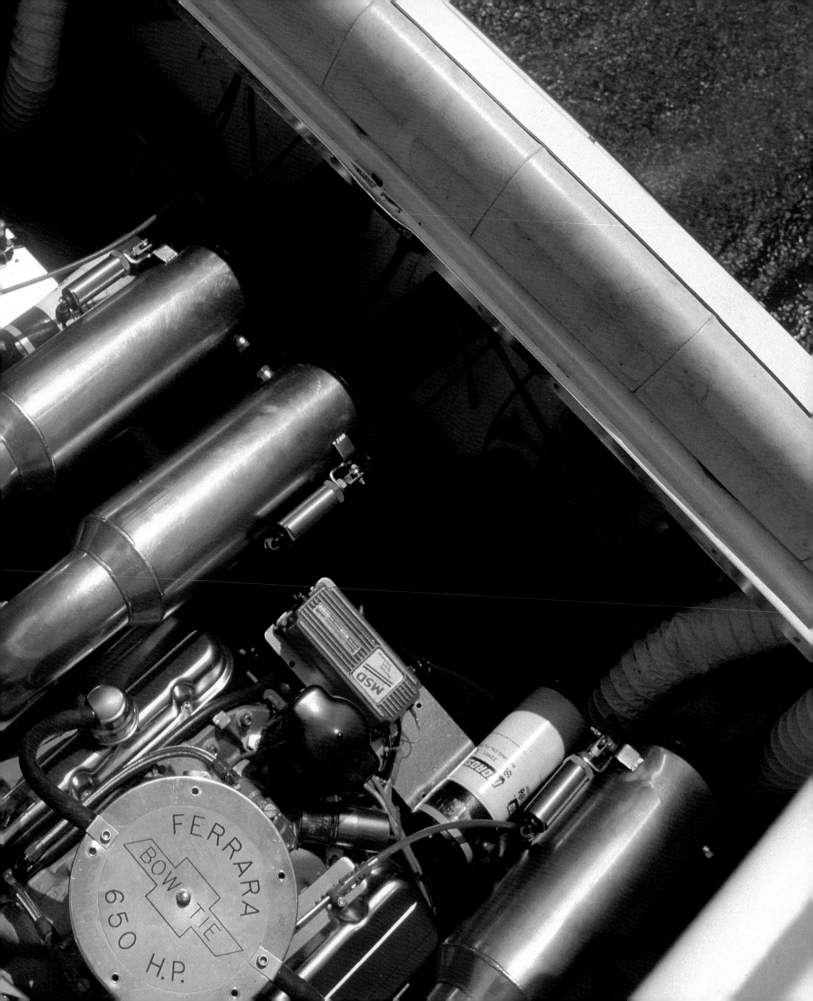

This photograph shows the sleek shapes of a Formula, silhouetted against the mangrove growth of Florida's Intracoastal Waterway. The Formula line of muscle boats is built by Thunderbird Products. Vic Porter, a veteran boat builder with roots in Decatur, Indiana, was instrumental in putting the Thunderbird organization in shape. In 1976, as the fruits of his efforts began to ripen, he bought the company, placing family members in many of the key management positions. The Formula boat was originally designed by Don Aronow, and his competition-proven deep-vee configuration stayed unchanged for twenty years. Today's Formulas—available in twenty-seven-, twenty-nine- and thirty-one-foot varieties—still conform to the original Aronow shape, with only minor changes. Porter and his family of boat builders are now returning to their Indiana roots—production at the Miami facility is being phased out in favor of a brand new plant in Decatur.

126